LET'S FIND OUT! SOCIAL STUDIES SKILLS

HOW DO YOU READ MAPS?

PHILIP WOLNY

Britannica® Educational Publishing

IN ASSOCIATION WITH

ROSEN EDUCATIONAL SERVICES

Published in 2019 by Britannica Educational Publishing (a trademark of Encyclopædia Britannica, Inc.) in association with The Rosen Publishing Group, Inc.
29 East 21st Street, New York, NY 10010

Distributed exclusively by Rosen Publishing.
To see additional Britannica Educational Publishing titles, go to rosenpublishing.com.

First Edition

Britannica Educational Publishing
J.E. Luebering: Executive Director, Core Editorial
Mary Rose McCudden: Editor, Britannica Student Encyclopedia

Rosen Publishing
Jane Katirgis: Editor
Brian Garvey: Series Designer
Ellina Litmanovich: Book Layout
Cindy Reiman: Photography Manager
Nicole DiMella: Photo Researcher

Library of Congress Cataloging-in-Publication Data

Names: Wolny, Philip, author.
Title: How do you read maps? / Philip Wolny.
Description: New York : Britannica Educational Publishing, in Association
with Rosen Educational Services, 2019 | Series: Let's find out! Social studies skills | Includes bibliographical references and index. | Audience: Grades 1–5.
Identifiers: LCCN 2018014216| ISBN 9781508107019 (library bound) | ISBN 9781508107200 (pbk.) | ISBN 9781508107361 (6 pack)
Subjects: LCSH: Map reading—Juvenile literature. | Maps—Juvenile literature.
Classification: LCC GA130 .W34 2018 | DDC 912.01/48—dc23
LC record available at https://lccn.loc.gov/2018014216

Manufactured in the United States of America

Photo credits: Cover KidStock/Blend Images/Getty Images; p. 4 Leigh/Shutterstock.com; p. 5 Robert Deutschman/The Image Bank /Getty Images; pp. 6, 16 Library of Congress Geography and Map Division; p. 7 shooarts/Shutterstock.com; p. 8 Art Alex/Shutterstock .com; p. 9 Bardocz Peter/Shutterstock.com; pp. 10, 18 © Encyclopædia Britannica, Inc.; p. 11 NOAA/National Weather Service; p. 12 DEA/A. De Gregorio/De Agostini Picture Library/Getty Images; p. 13 Encyclopaedia Britannica/Universal Images Group/Getty Images; p. 14 Peter Hermes Furian/Shutterstock.com; p. 15 Cartarium/Shutterstock.com; p. 17 Monkey Business Images/Thinkstock; pp. 19, 24 zlatovlaska2008/Shutterstock.com; p. 20 Bardocz Peter/Shutterstock.com; p. 21 s-c-s/iStock/Thinkstock; p. 22 Courtesy of the University of Texas Libraries, The University of Texas at Austin.; p. 23 Sergei Fadeichev/TASS/Getty Images; p. 25 Trevor Chriss/Alamy Stock Photo; p. 26 OlegDoroshin/Shutterstock.com; p. 27 CL-Medien/Shutterstock.com; p. 28 wonderlandstock/Alamy Stock Photo; p. 29 Hero Images/DigitalVision/Getty Images; interior pages background Aris Suwanmalee/Shutterstock.com.

Contents

What Are Maps?

Suppose you want to find your way around a new neighborhood or school, the country, or the world. A map is

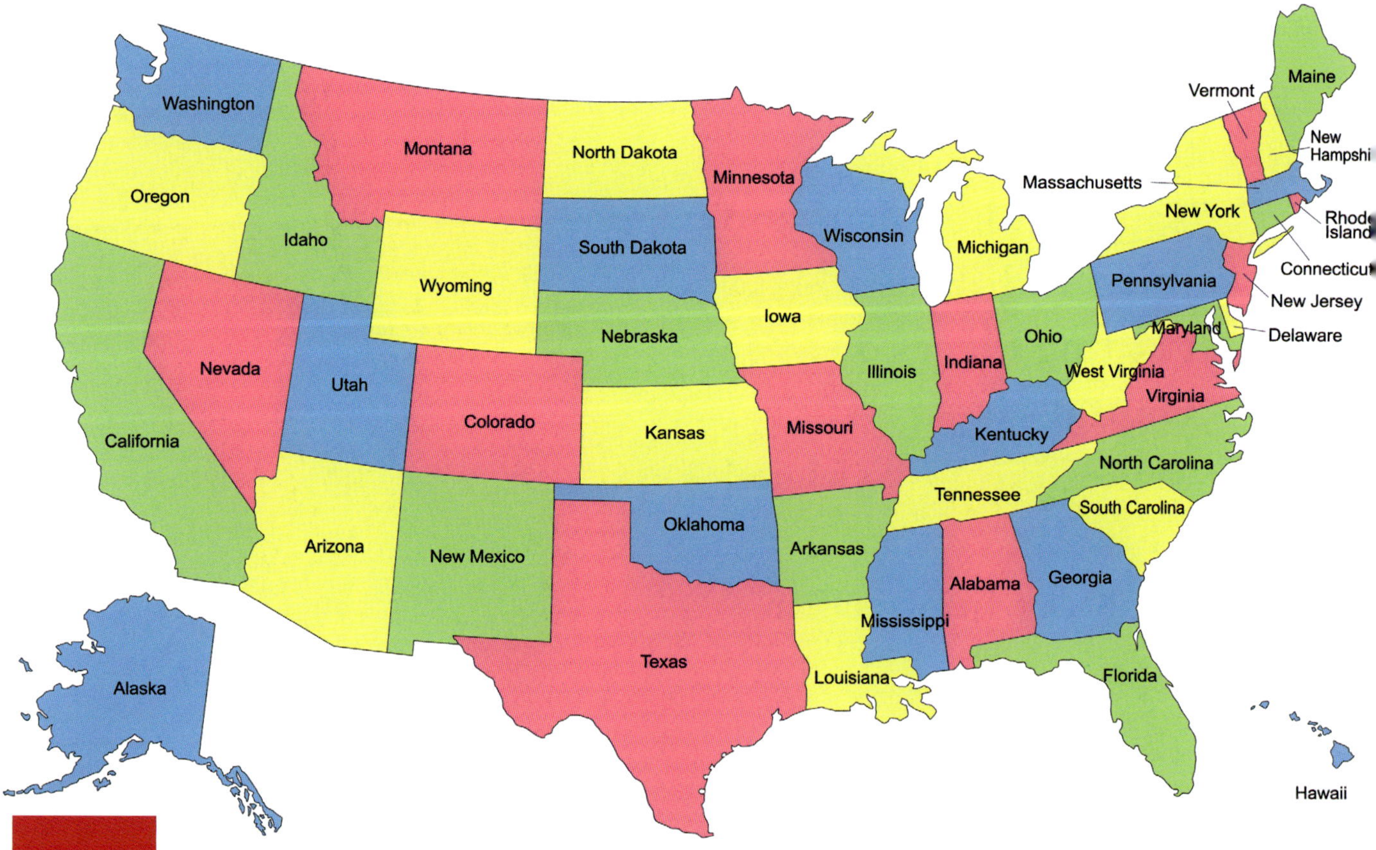

Many maps and globes show invisible boundaries, including those between nations.

an easy way to discover where things are! Imagine how hard it would be to travel to a new place without a map.

A map is a drawing of all or part of Earth's surface. Most maps are drawn on a flat surface. A map displayed on a round surface is called a globe. Globes give the same kinds of information that flat maps do. Because Earth is almost round, a globe represents it best. A globe shows Earth as it looks when seen from space.

THINK ABOUT IT

Can you name other invisible things that can be shown on a map?

Maps may show visible features, such as rivers, forests, buildings, and roads. They also may show things that cannot be seen, such as where one state is separated from the states around it. Special maps show other invisible things, like weather patterns. No matter the type, maps give us lots of information.

This map of the United States shows all fifty states.

This world map is an example of a political map.

Two common kinds of maps are topographic maps and political maps. Topographic maps show the location and shape of features on Earth's surface. These features often are natural things, such as mountains and lakes. Topographic maps also can show things that humans have built, such as roads and railroads.

Political maps show the boundaries of countries, states, provinces, counties, and cities. Boundaries are the unseen lines that separate places run by different governments. Some visible features, like rivers and mountain ranges, also can act as boundaries. These features physically separate one place from another.

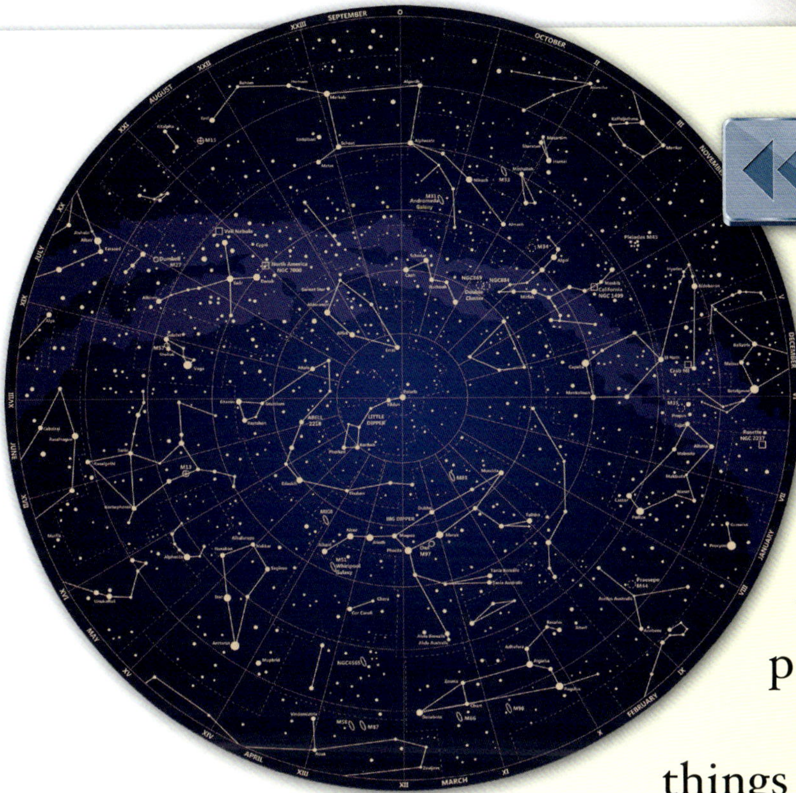

A star map is useful for science students, scientists, and people who look at stars as a hobby.

Most maps combine features of both topographic and political maps.

Some special maps show things that are not on Earth's surface. For example, star maps show the stars in all or part of the sky. Transportation maps, like subway or underground railway maps, show things that may be all or partly underground.

Compare and Contrast

How are political maps similar to topographic maps? How are they different?

Showing Direction

Many maps have a symbol called a compass rose. This symbol got its name from its shape, which looks like a flower. Arrows or pointers stick out from the center, like petals. These arrows show the **cardinal directions**—north, east, south, and west.

Some maps have compass roses showing northeast, southeast, southwest, and northwest. These points are called the intercardinal directions. This name comes from the prefix "inter," meaning "between." It refers to a direction between two of the cardinal directions. Other maps lack a compass rose. Instead, they may have just an arrow pointing north.

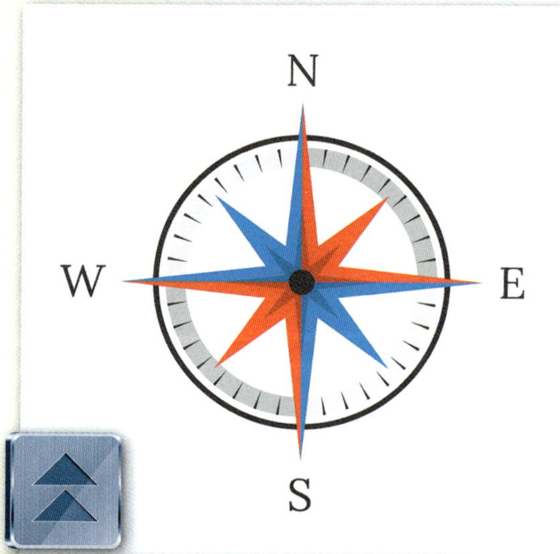

This compass rose shows the four main directions.

The compass rose in the upper right-hand corner of this map helps map readers to figure out where places are located.

Maps often are printed so that north is at the top, but that is not always the case. Therefore, the compass rose helps map users to figure out which way is which. The relationship between directions on a map and directions in the real world is known as orientation.

Vocabulary

The cardinal directions are the main points on a compass. In clockwise order, they are north, east, south, and west.

Map Legends

A legend is a list that describes the symbols used on a map. It is sometimes called a key. A map key helps you to unlock the meaning of symbols and other visual aids, including colors.

Mapmakers use legends or keys to explain important information on a map. Most of the time, a map legend can be found in a separate box or on the side of a map. It often shows symbols and colors

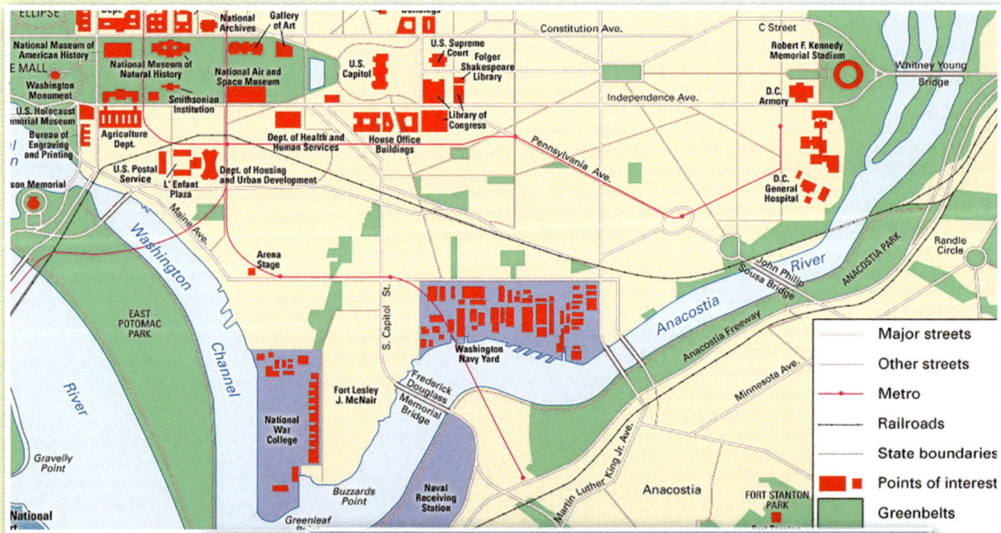

The legend on this map of Washington, DC, helps users to spot roads, parks, and important places.

The legend on the right side of this map shows that each color stands for an amount of rainfall.

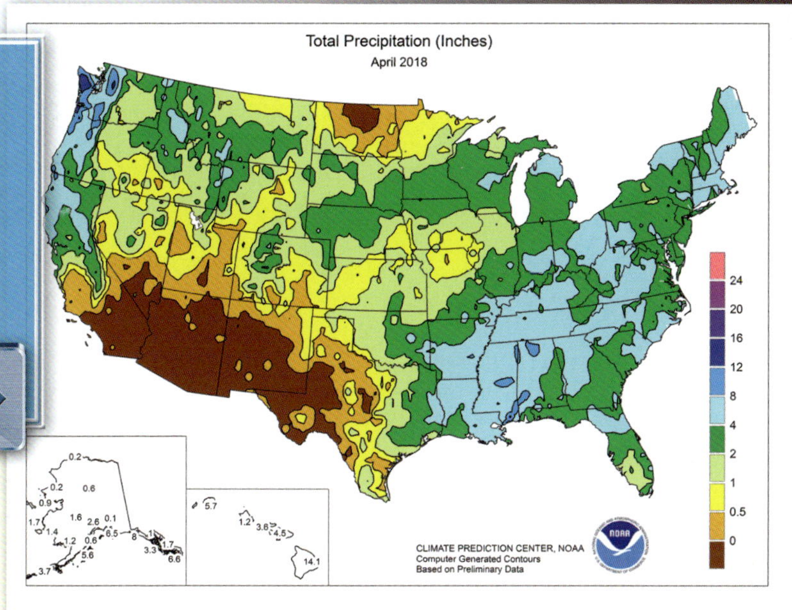

on the left and definitions on the right. For example, the legend on a map of Washington, DC, might have dots and squares next to labels. The labels could explain that dots mean train stops and squares mean places to visit.

Different types of maps have different types of legends. The legend for a map of a park might have symbols for paths and picnic areas. The legend for a weather map might have a range of colors for different amounts of rainfall.

Think About It

Would you be able to figure out what a map was showing without a map legend or key?

Map Symbols

In the past, mapmakers used drawings to show where things such as castles and mountains were located. The drawings were large so they could be seen clearly. Such artwork was nice to look at and easy to understand. However, it produced maps that were cluttered and not very detailed. Over time, mapmakers made maps less fancy. They replaced pictures with symbols.

On modern maps, symbols are made of simple shapes and lines. Each symbol represents a particular thing. A single black line might stand for a road. Double black lines might stand for a highway.

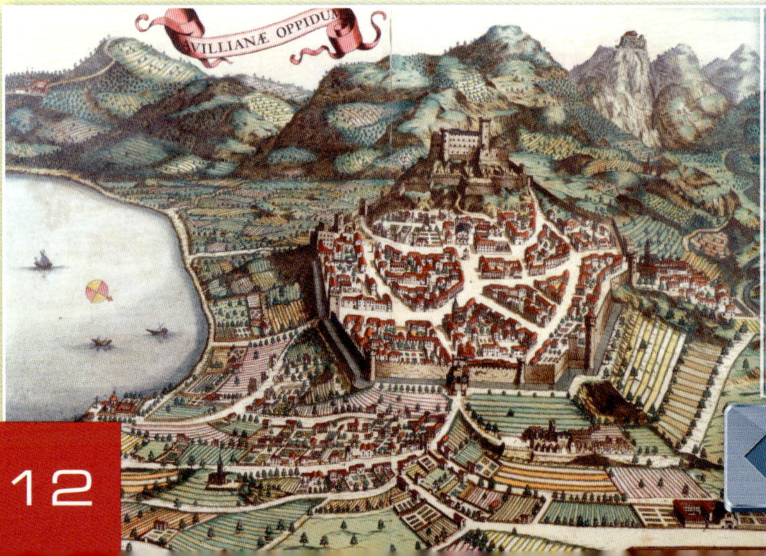

This map of a town in Italy is from the 1700s. It uses detailed drawings instead of symbols.

Symbols for natural features have unique shapes and patterns. Mountains are sometimes shown as triangles or as upside-down "V" shapes. Forest symbols may look like groups of tiny trees or green patches. A scattering of dots is a common symbol for deserts.

Good symbols stand out from the background of the map. They are easy to tell apart and easy to understand.

This map of California uses different symbols for aqueducts, canals, and dams.

Think About It

What natural or man-made features might have similar symbols? How might a mapmaker make it easy to tell them apart?

Map Colors

Maps can use color to mark different areas or features. Maps often use the colors we usually think of when we imagine natural features. For example, what color reminds you of water? You probably thought of blue. On a map, rivers, lakes, oceans, and other bodies of water are usually shown in blue. Light brown or tan often shows where deserts are.

On this map of Florida, land is shown in light colors. Bodies of water (such as the Gulf of Mexico and the Atlantic Ocean) are colored blue.

Colors also can be used to show invisible or unseen qualities. A population map might use darker colors to mark where more people live. Lighter colors would show where fewer people live.

Maps that show countries, states, or other political features often use bright colors and bold lines. This type of design makes it easy to find different places on the map.

Using many colors is a good way to show political boundaries.

Compare and Contrast

If you were making a map of your school, which colors and symbols would you use? Which colors and symbols would you use for a map of your town or country?

SCALE

A map is always smaller than the area it represents. Most maps include something called a scale to show how

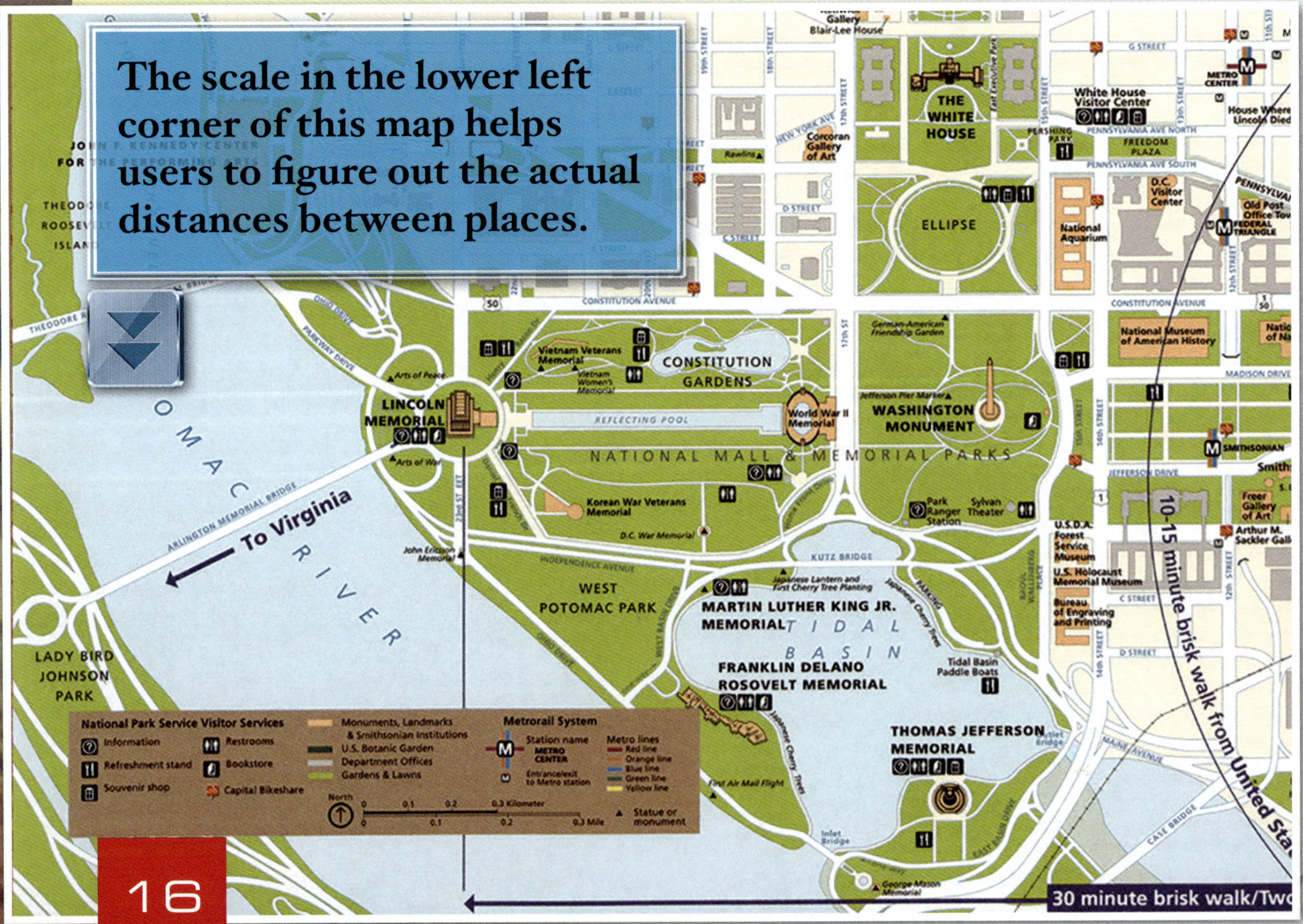

The scale in the lower left corner of this map helps users to figure out the actual distances between places.

much smaller the map is. The scale shows how distances on the map are related to the actual distances.

VOCABULARY

The distance around Earth, a globe, or any other sphere is known as its circumference.

Map scale can be shown in different ways. The simplest way is a graphic scale. A graphic scale is a ruled line or bar that is usually marked off in miles or kilometers. A graphic scale can be used to measure distances on the map. Some maps have a verbal scale. A verbal scale uses words, such as "one inch equals 60 miles."

Compared to most maps, globes show a much larger area—the entire surface of Earth. The **circumference** of many globes is 3.14 feet (0.96 meter). The circumference of Earth is 24,902 miles (40,075 km). Because globes are so much smaller than the area they represent, they are said to have a small scale.

Globes have a small scale. On a globe, an inch can represent hundreds of miles.

POLITICAL MAPS

You may have seen a sign along the road, such as "Welcome to Colorado," when you entered a new state. Perhaps the sign was the only thing that showed the state line. Some places are separated by rivers or other natural features. Others are separated by walls or fences.

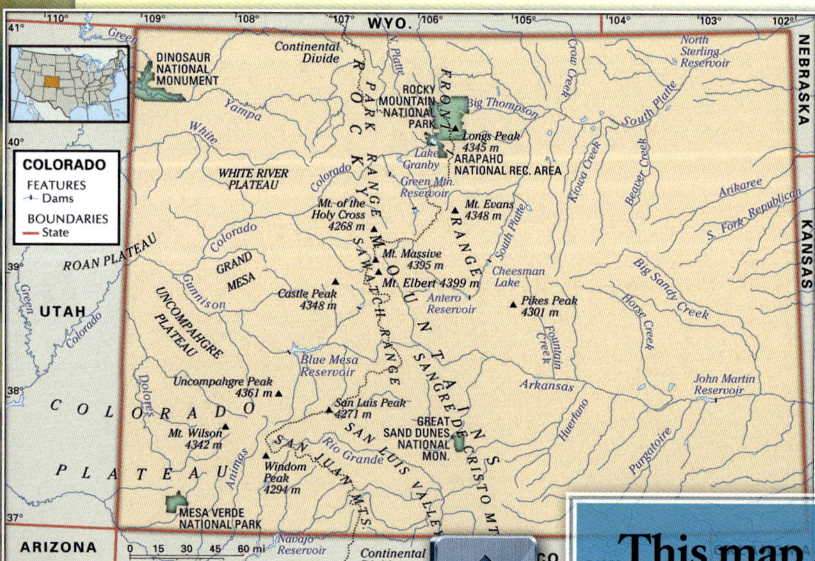

This map shows Colorado and several states that border it.

But many places are separated only by imaginary lines.

Political maps show these invisible borders. They show where one country or state is separated

The sections on this map indicate the borders of the provinces of Canada.

from its neighbors. They also may show other government boundaries, such as lines that divide states into counties or districts.

Besides borders, political maps give us detailed information about a place, including its cities and towns. Dots show where cities are located. Dots for major cities are often bigger than those for smaller cities. A star symbol is often used to mark a capital city.

Compare and Contrast

How would a political map of the United States be similar to a map of North America? How would it be different?

Topographic Maps and Globes

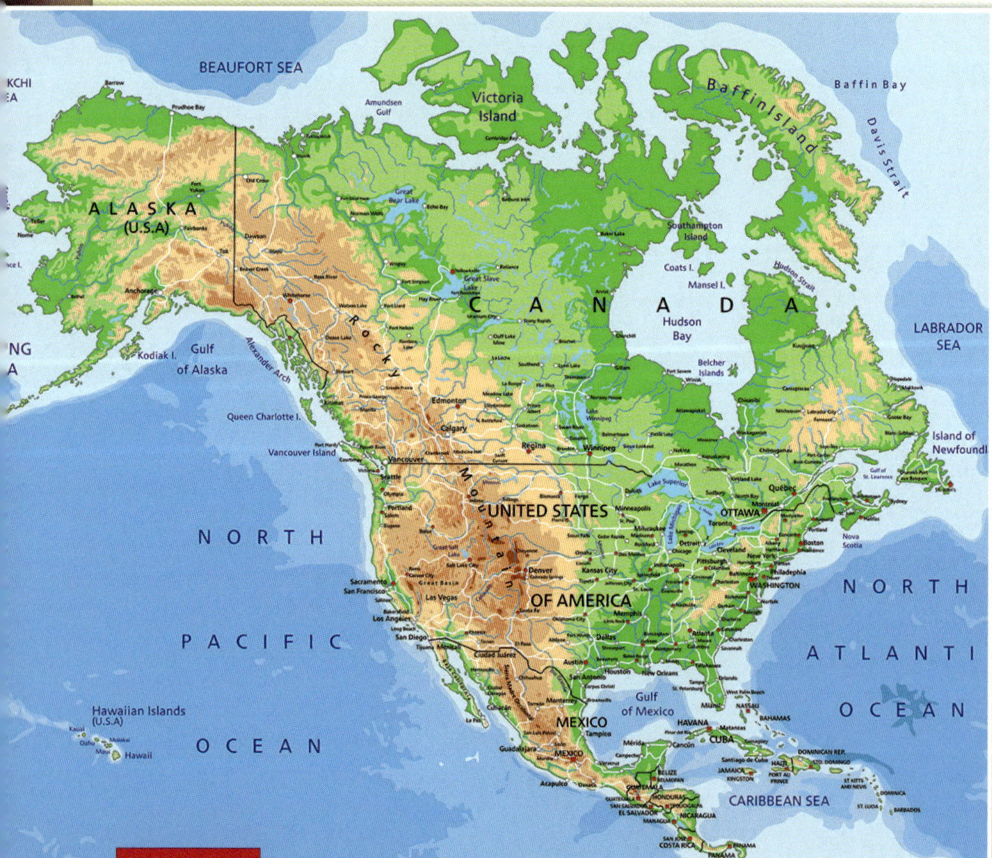

You now know that political maps can show invisible features of places. Topographic maps, on the other hand, show the visible features of

Compare and Contrast

Which symbols might be used only on a topographic map? Which symbols might be used on both political and topographic maps?

Earth. These features include natural things you can see, like rivers, lakes, mountains, hills, deserts, forests, and other plant life. They also include visible features that are man-made, like roads, railroads, and walls.

Areas of Earth that are underwater also have natural shapes that can be mapped. Some topographic maps and globes show physical features found under the oceans and other bodies of water. This type of topographic map is useful to scientists and sailors.

Many topographic maps include symbols for things that are usually shown on political maps. These symbols help people to see where natural features like mountains are, in relation to man-made things like highways and state borders.

This topographic map of North America shows where major physical features of the continent are located.

Road and Transit Maps

Some of the most commonly used maps are ones that help people to get around. At one time or another, almost everyone has to drive or take public transportation somewhere.

The main purpose of road maps is to provide drivers and other travelers with information on how to get somewhere using streets, roads, and highways.

This road map shows major highways in the United States.

A subway map helps riders to figure out which trains they need to take to their destination.

Different colors and designs in a road map's legend usually mark different kinds of motorways. Some may be toll roads that require a toll, or fee, to drive on them.

Think About It

How could a highway map help you to plan a road trip?

Many cities, large towns, and counties have their own public transportation systems. Systems in very large cities might have dozens of different bus, train, or tramway lines. Maps of these systems often are color coded to help passengers make choices about where to get on and off a bus or train. They also can help riders figure out where bus lines and train lines meet.

Finding Places on a Map

Many maps use a system called latitude and longitude. Latitude and longitude are sets of imaginary lines that circle Earth. Latitude runs east and west. Longitude runs north and south. Any place can be found on a map using its measurements of both latitude and longitude.

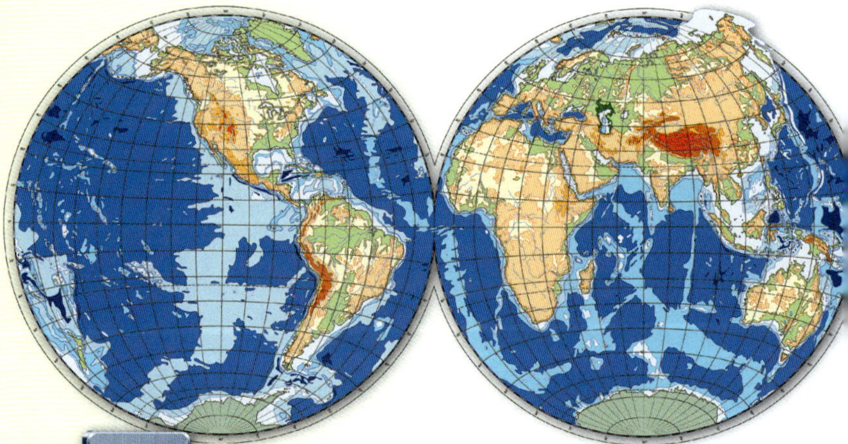

You can find any specific spot on Earth by knowing its exact latitude and longitude measurements.

Lines in a checkerboard pattern are called a grid. Map readers use coordinates on a grid to find specific places on a map.

Some maps are divided into sections like squares on a checkerboard. Rows across may be lettered "A," "B," "C," and so on. Columns that go up and down may be numbered "1," "2," "3," and so on. These maps often have an index that tells where to find a place by using the letters and numbers. If the index says a place is located at "B 2," for example, the place can be found where row "B" and column "2" cross. Road maps often use this system. People sometimes call these crossing points **coordinates**.

VOCABULARY

The **coordinates** of a place are a set of numbers (or a combination of numbers and letters) that tell a map user where exactly the place is on a map.

Digital Maps

Many of the maps we use today are digital maps. People can look at digital maps on computers, laptops, and smartphones. Online digital maps are useful in many ways.

The information on many digital maps comes from satellites orbiting Earth. Satellites take detailed pictures of streets and neighborhoods that are used in many

Digital maps can be a great help to drivers and other travelers, especially in places they have not visited before.

The internet company Google uses cars like this one to take pictures of the streets in many areas. Google uses these pictures in its digital map programs.

digital maps. Some digital maps also use pictures taken by cars that drive around on Earth's surface. Such pictures are useful because they show you exactly what a place looks like.

One of the most popular uses of online maps is to get directions. When you enter an address or street intersection, the map program tells you how to get there. On many digital maps, you can pick whether you are walking, driving, biking, or using buses or trains.

Think About It

What might be a good reason to have a paper map on hand, even if digital maps seem easier to use?

Make Your Own Maps!

A good way to learn about maps is to make your own. You can start by picking a few places in your town or city that are important. Include your home, school, and other places that matter to you.

Make a legend. Draw some symbols or simple pictures that represent buildings, parks, and other destinations. Then bike, walk, or have a family member drive you to these places to figure out how to get to them. Draw the roads you took on your map. Next, using the symbols you made, mark your destinations on the map.

Drawing maps can be fun. Making your own maps also can teach you about your neighborhood or town.

Compare and Contrast

How would a map made by a kid who lives in a big city differ from one made by a kid who lives in a small town? How would they be similar?

For a challenge, add cardinal directions to your map. Take a walk around the neighborhood. Keep track of which way the streets turn. Use a compass if possible to track which streets go north, south, east, or west. Then you can make your own compass rose and put it on your map.

To show what you have learned about maps, share the map you drew with someone. Can that person use your map to find places around your home?

Using maps in the real world—for example, while hiking somewhere in your area—can be exciting and fun.

Glossary

border An outer part or edge of a place or area, such as a country or a state.

boundary Something that shows a limit or end; a dividing line.

cluttered Messy or confusing to look at.

compass A device with a magnetic needle that points north.

digital Characterized by electronic and computerized technology.

intercardinal Referring to directions between the cardinal directions, such as northeast and southwest.

key Another word for a map legend.

latitude An imaginary line that runs east and west around Earth; a distance measured north or south from the equator.

longitude An imaginary line that runs north and south around Earth, through the North and South Poles; a distance measured east or west from the prime meridian (a longitude line that runs through England).

man-made Made by people rather than nature.

orientation The relationship between directions on a map and your directional position in reality.

political Referring to a map that shows the boundaries of countries, states, provinces, counties, and cities.

province A large division of a country having its own government.

specialized Designed with a special purpose in mind.

sphere A three-dimensional object that is completely round.

topographic Describes a map that shows Earth's natural features.

tramway A form of public street transportation that runs on rails and is often powered by overhead electric cables.

For More Information

Books

Besel, Jennifer M. *Types of Maps*. North Mankato, MN: Capstone Press, 2014.

Bluthenthal, Todd. *Making Maps.* New York, NY: Gareth Stevens Publishing, 2018.

Boswell, Kelly. *Maps, Maps, Maps!* North Mankato, MN: Capstone Press, 2014.

Hirsch, Rebecca E. *Using Political Maps*. Minneapolis, MN: Lerner Publications, 2017.

Matzke, Ann H. *Reading Maps.* Vero Beach, FL: Rourke Educational Media, 2014.

Websites

Kids Geo
https://kidsgeo.com/?s=Maps

National Geographic Kids: World Map
https://kids.nationalgeographic.com/world

PBS Kids: The Cat in the Hat Can Map This and That
http://pbskids.org/catinthehat/games/the-cat-in-the-hat-can-map-this-and-that

Index